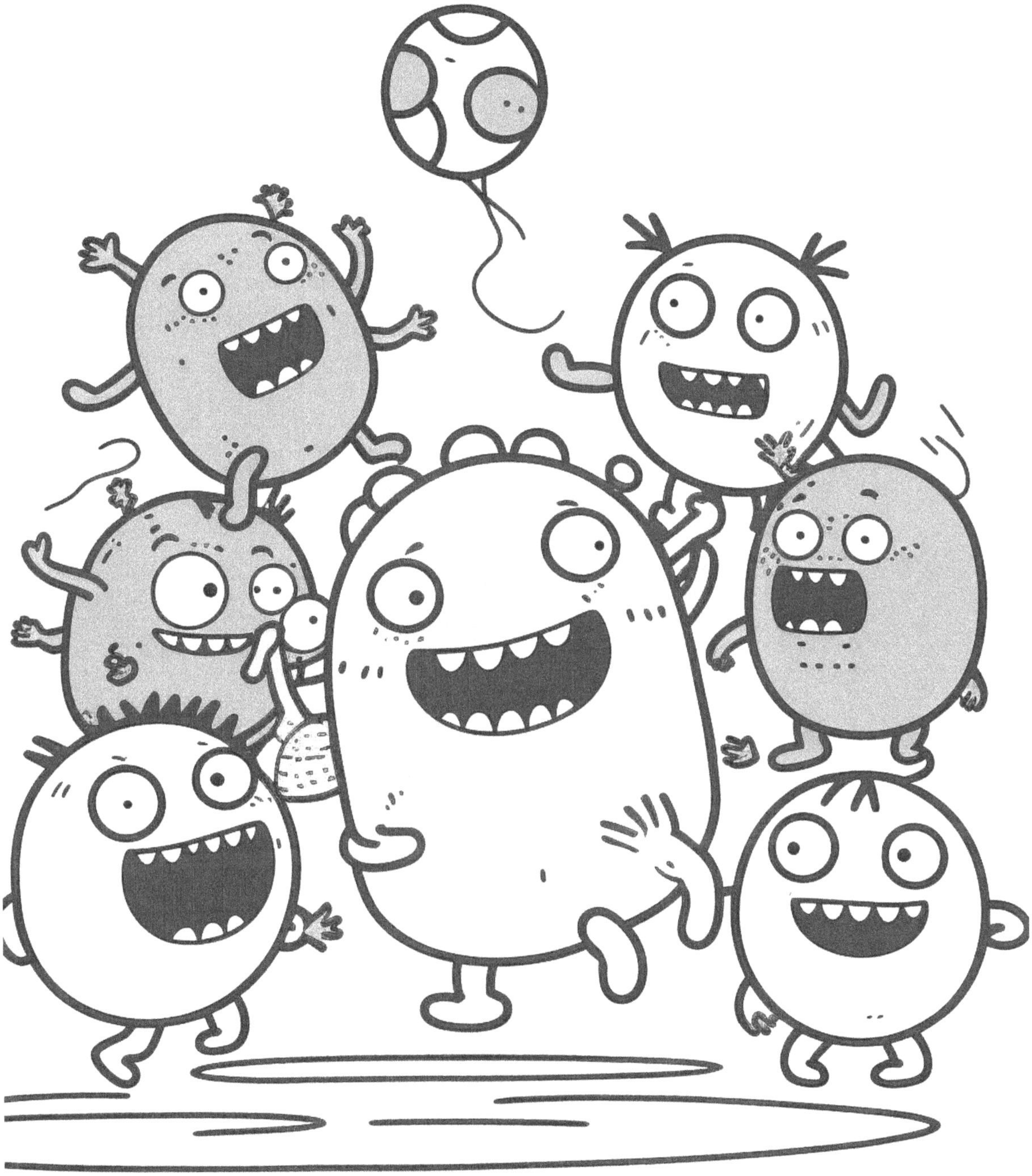

THIS COLORING BOOK
BELONGS TO:

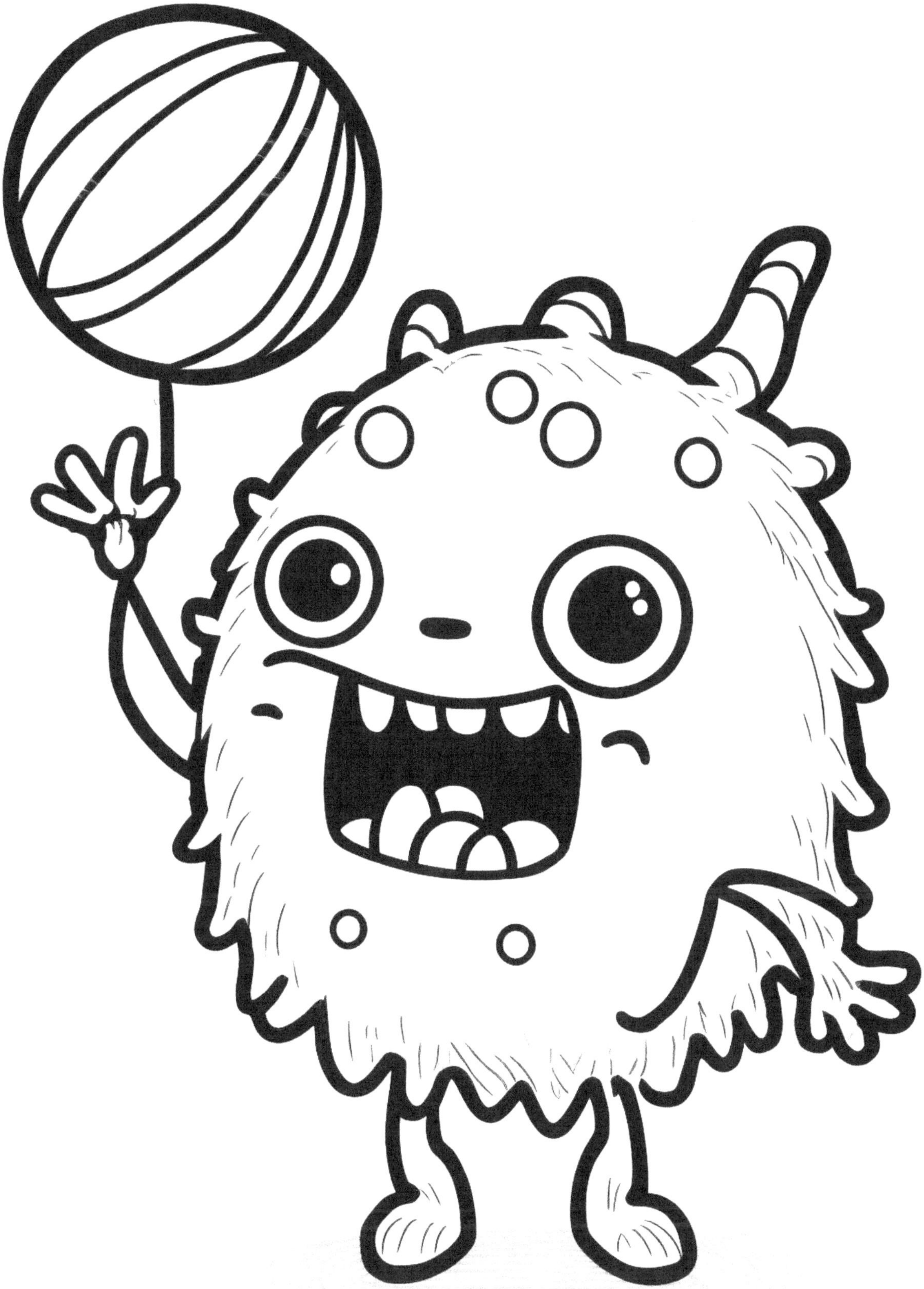

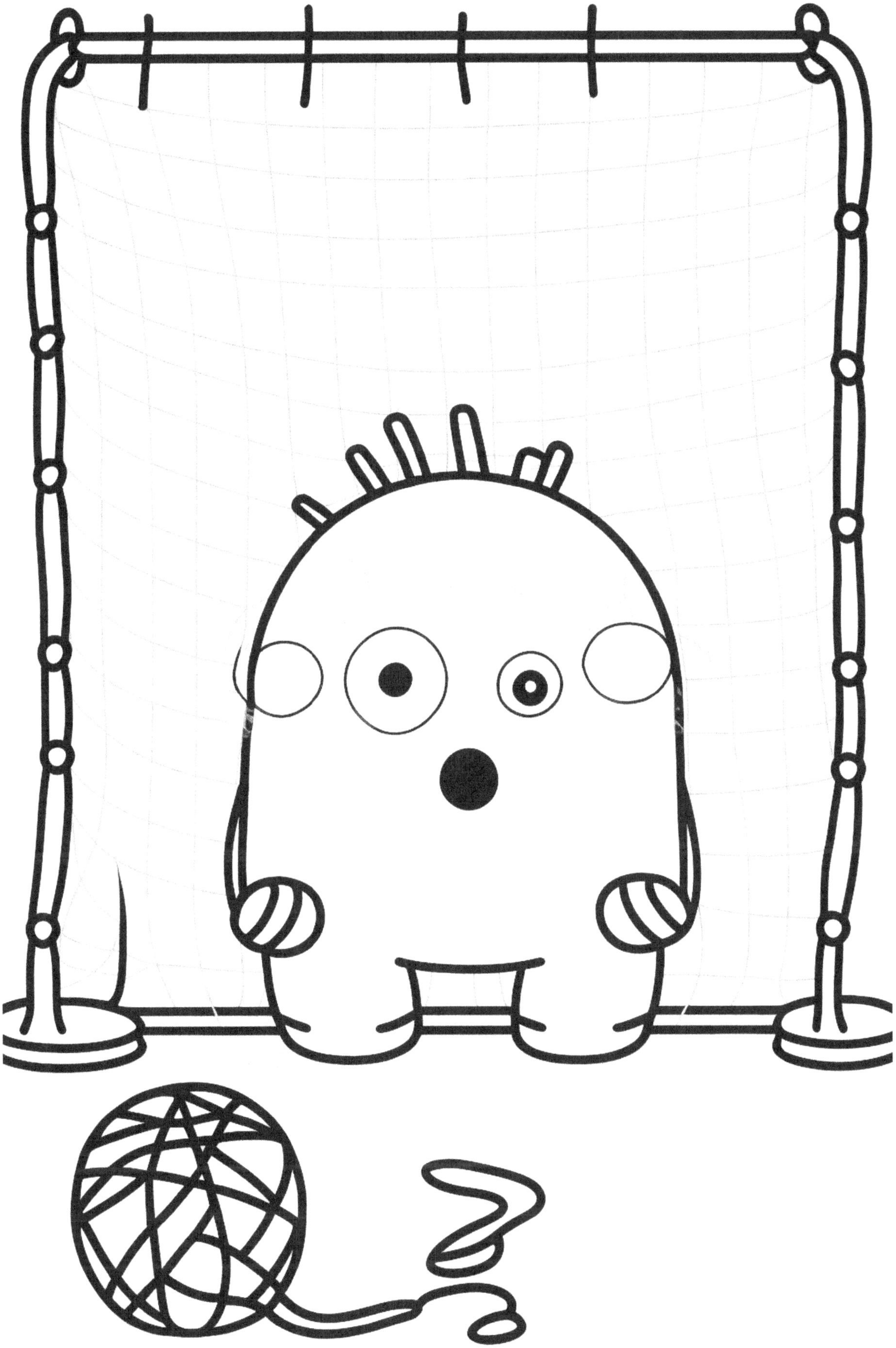

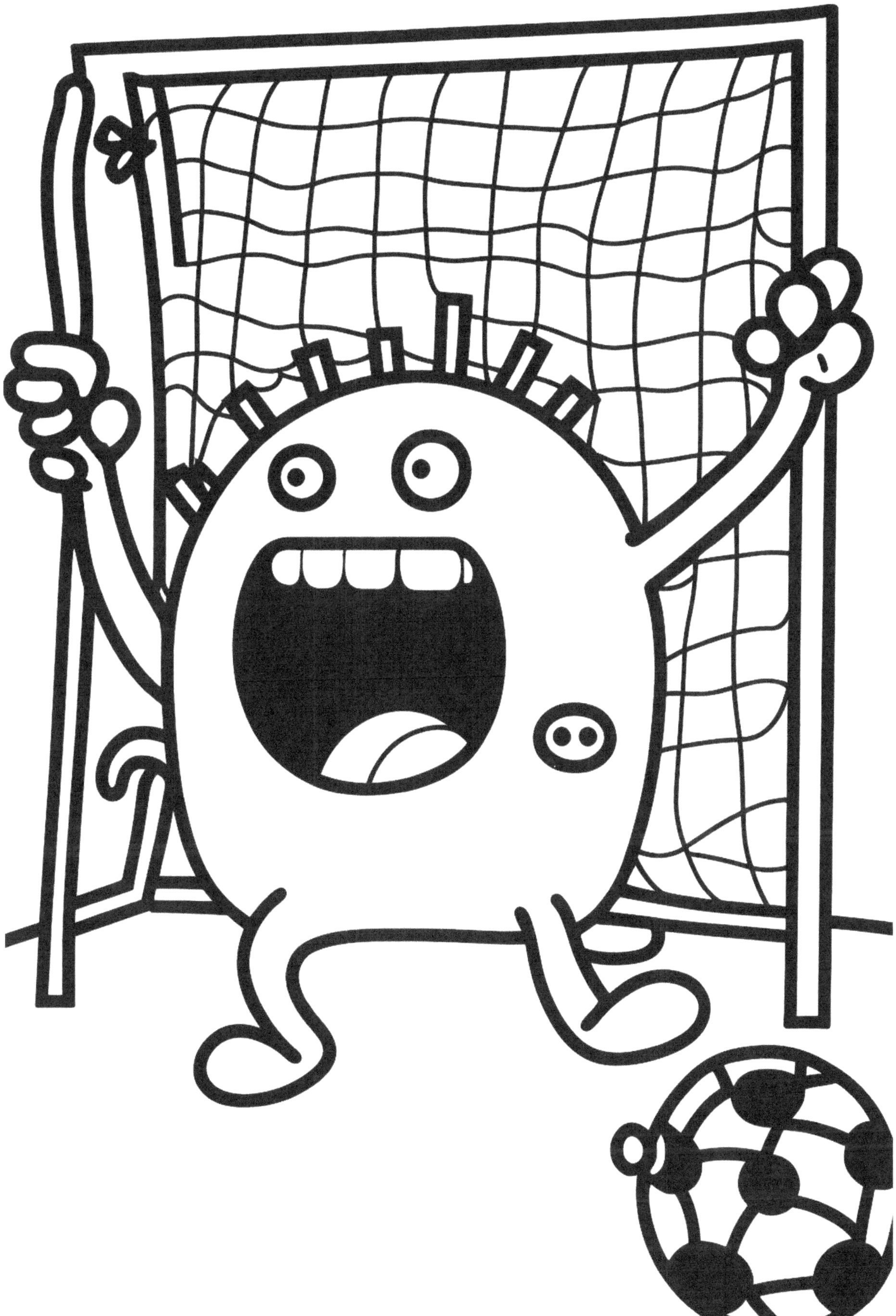

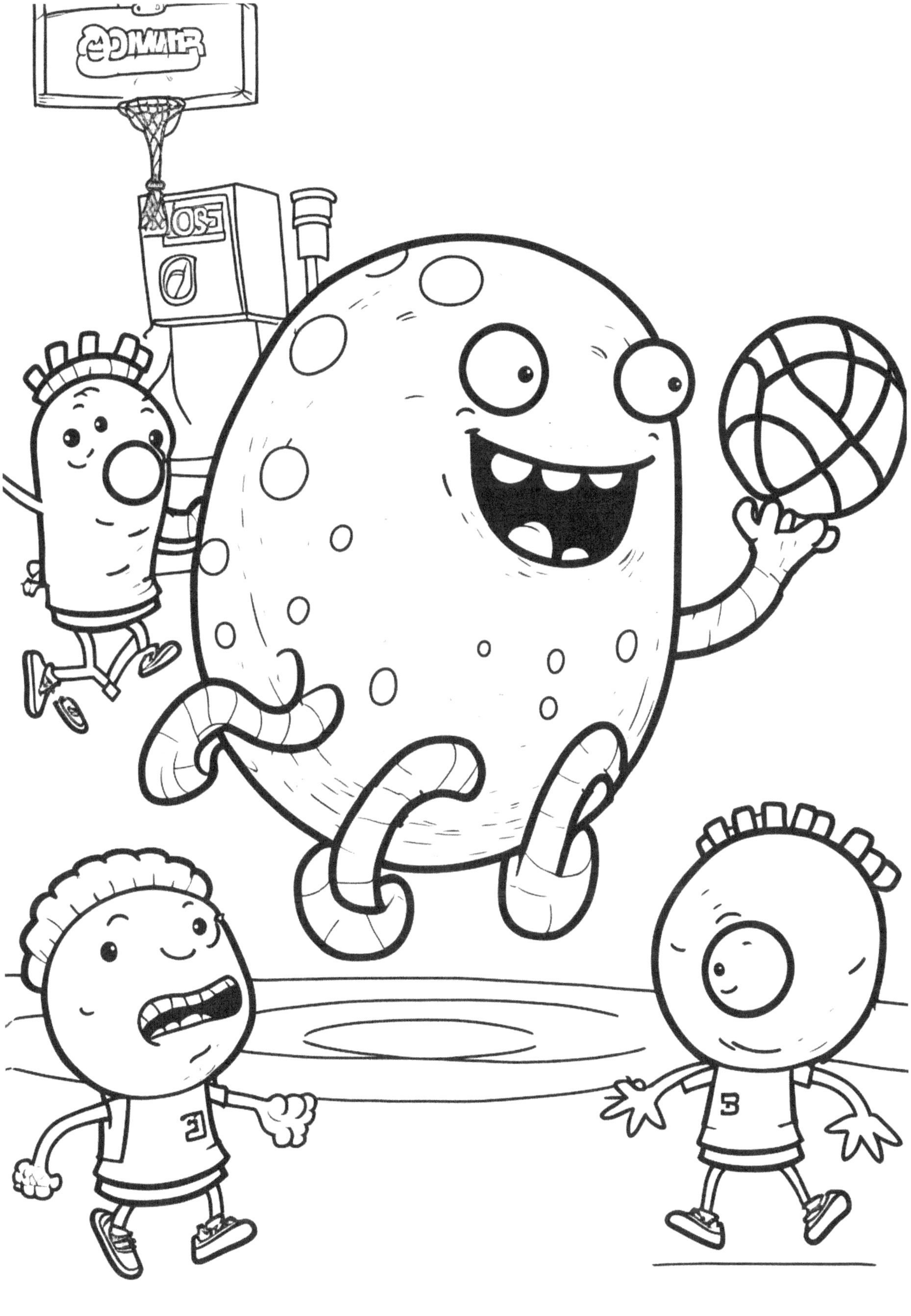

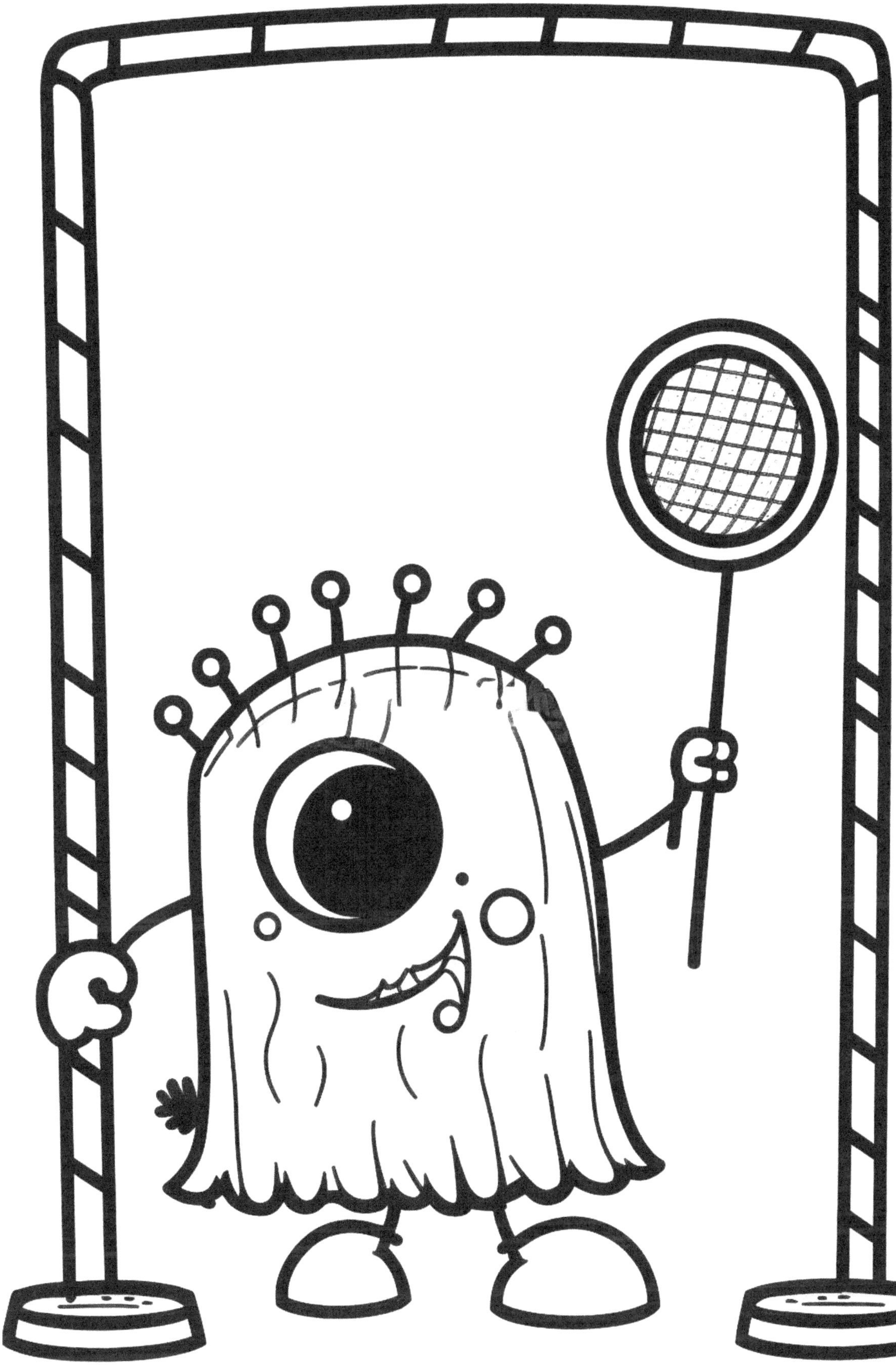

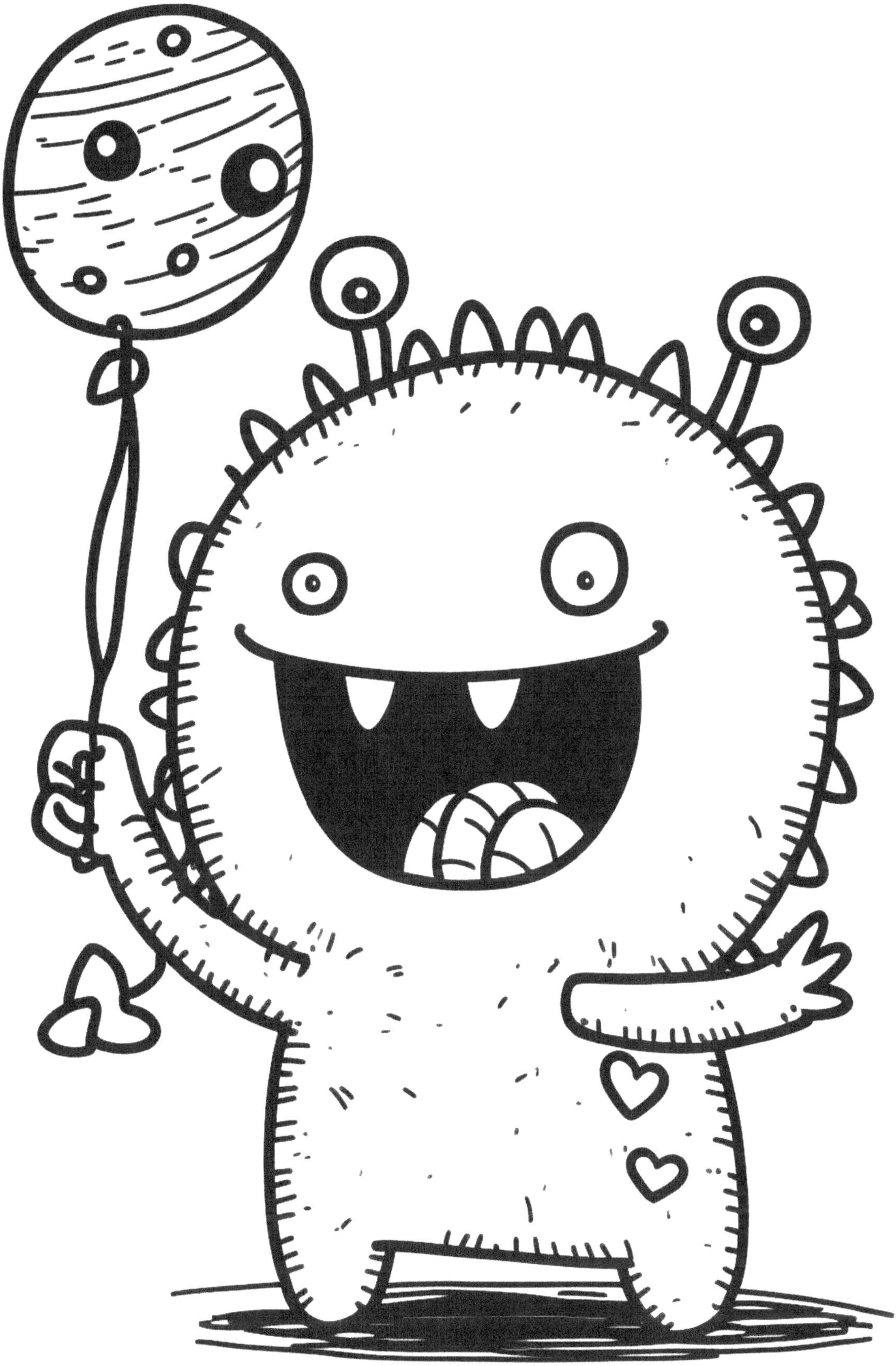

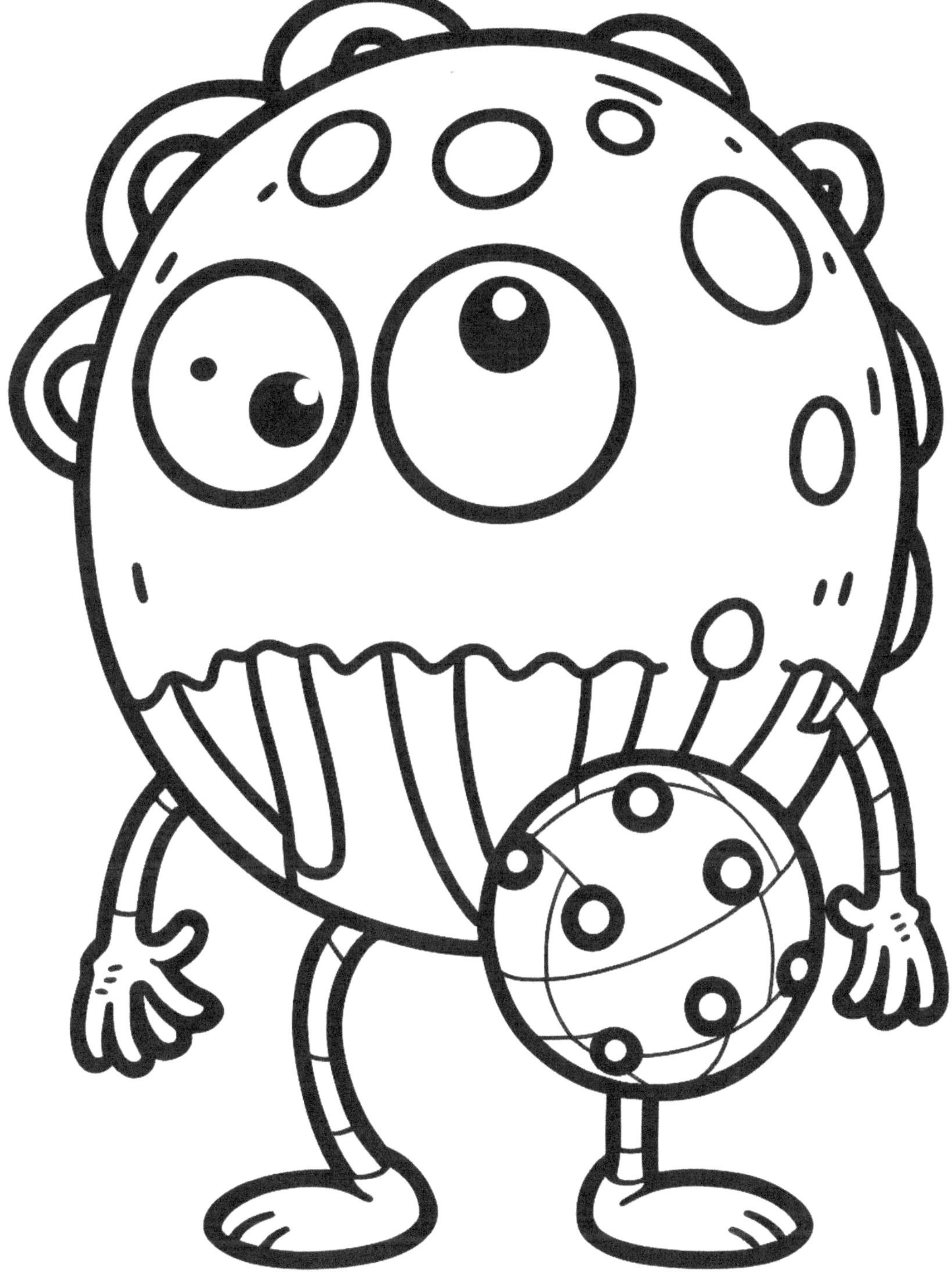

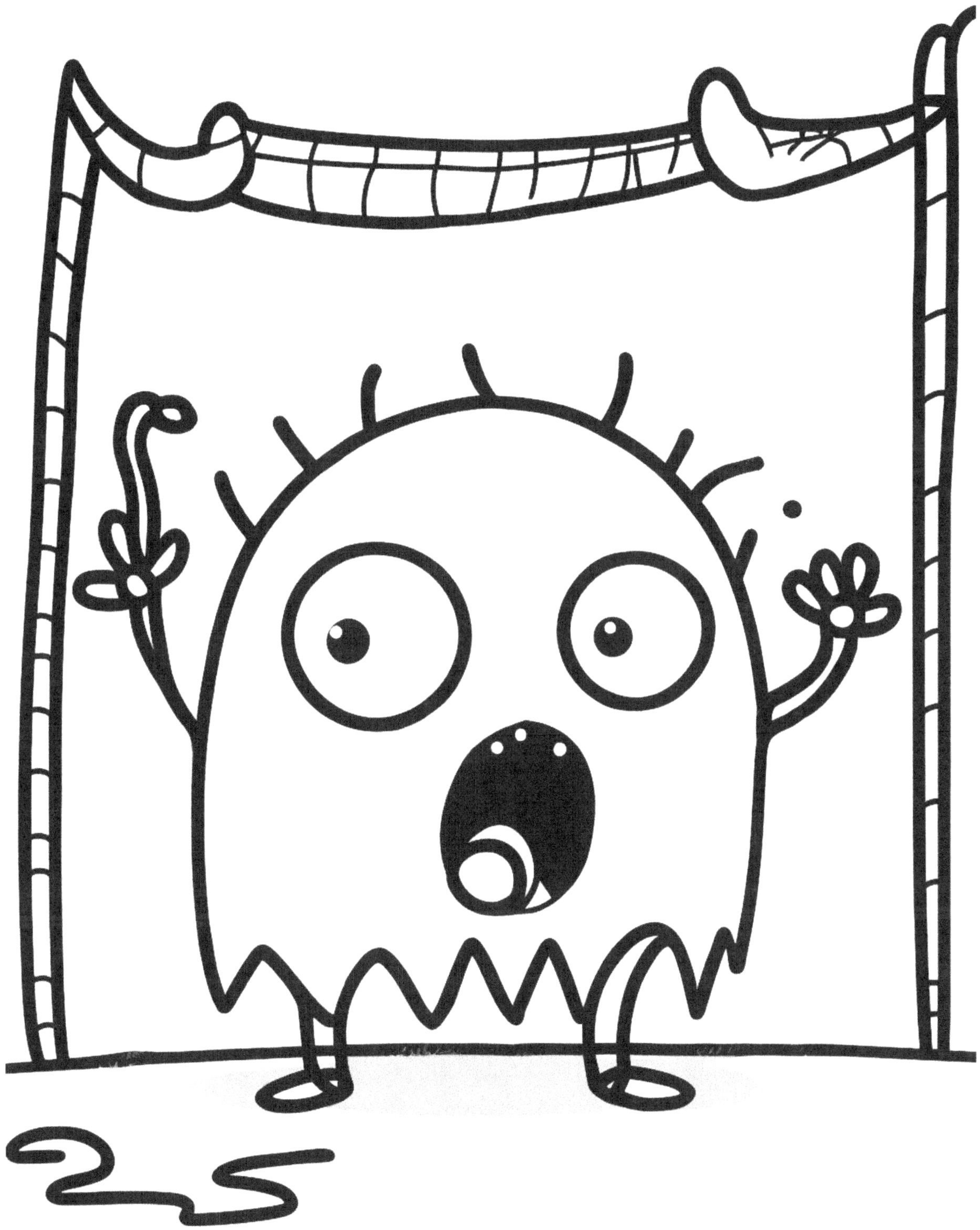

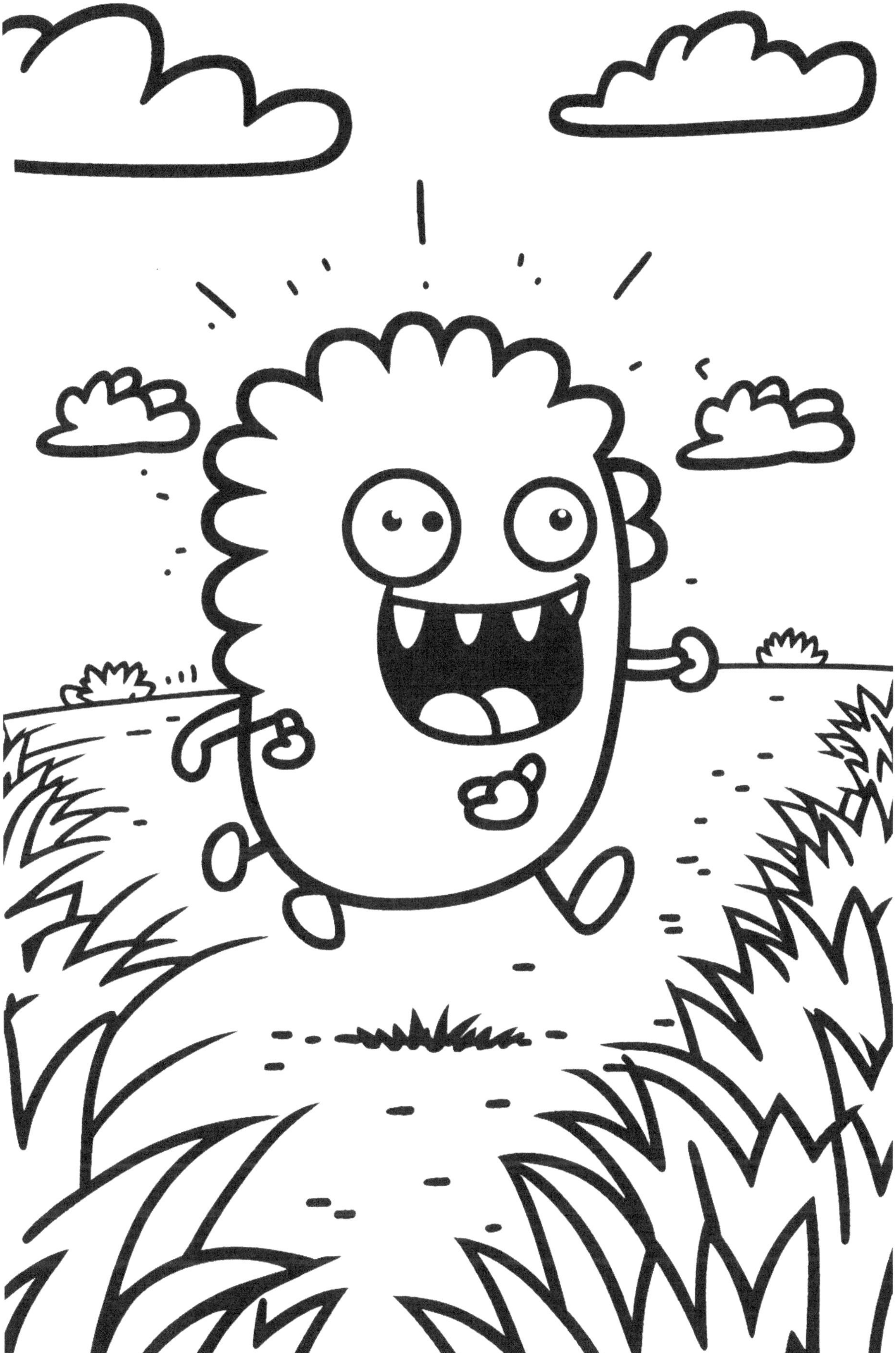

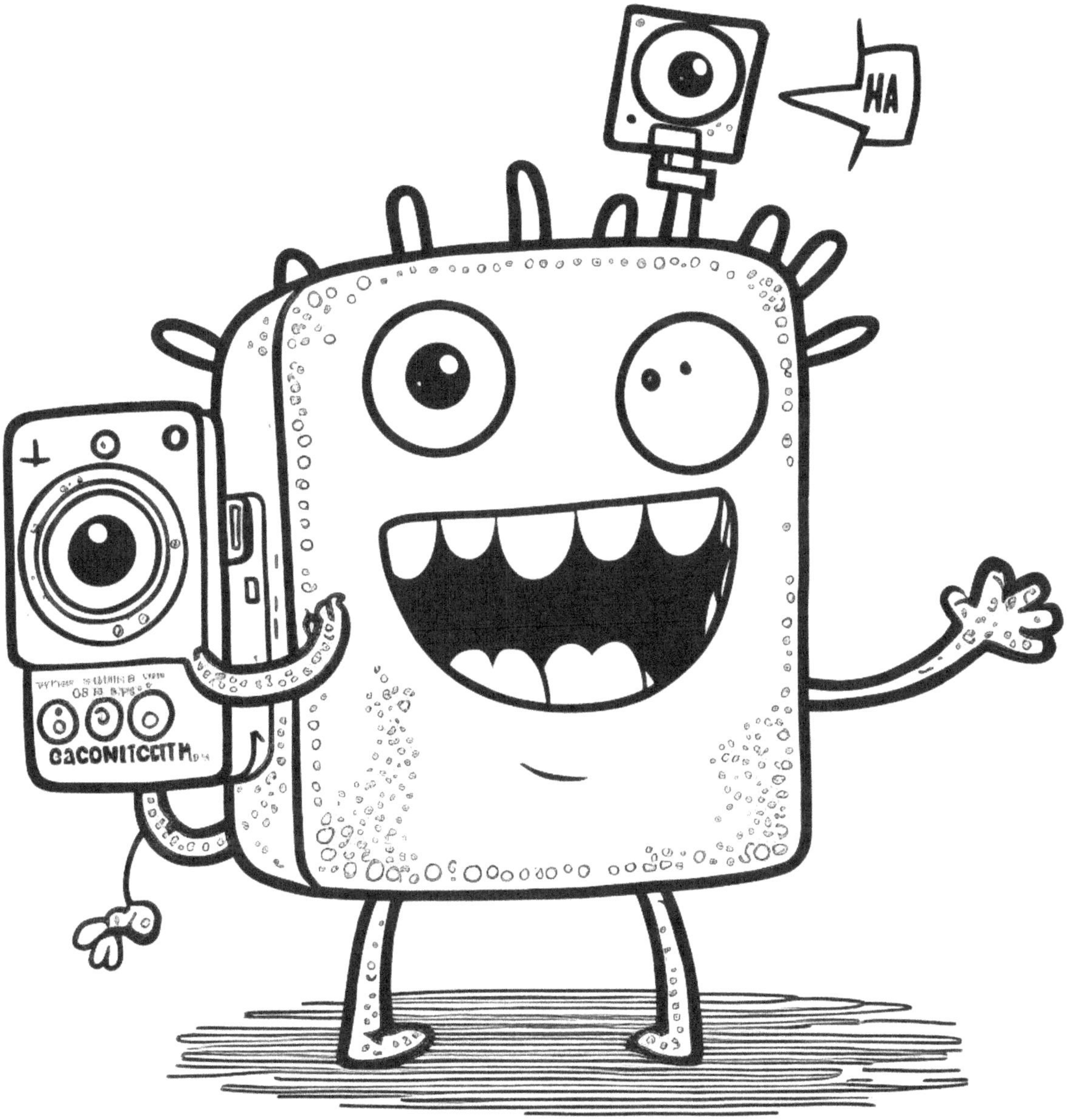
HA

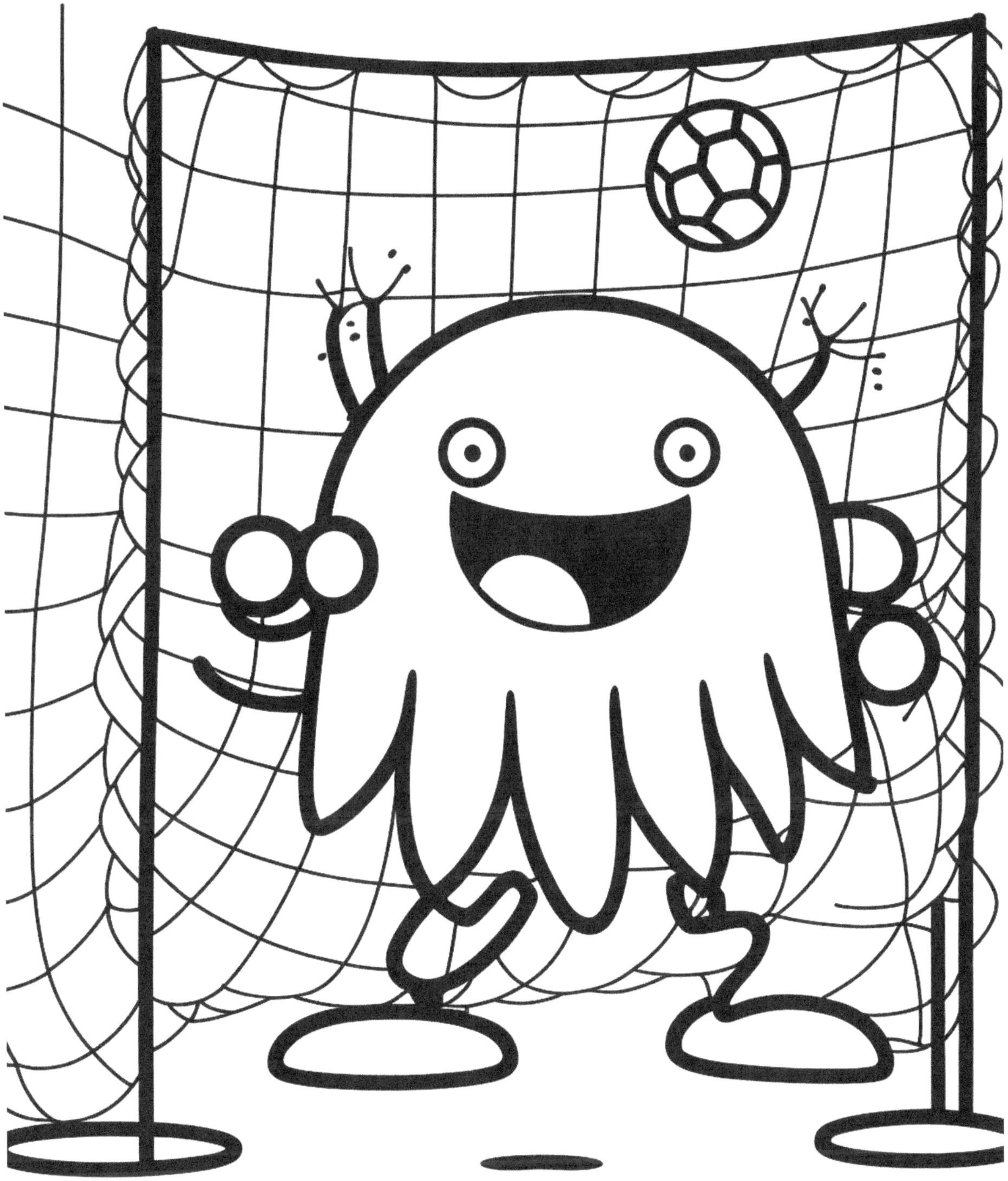

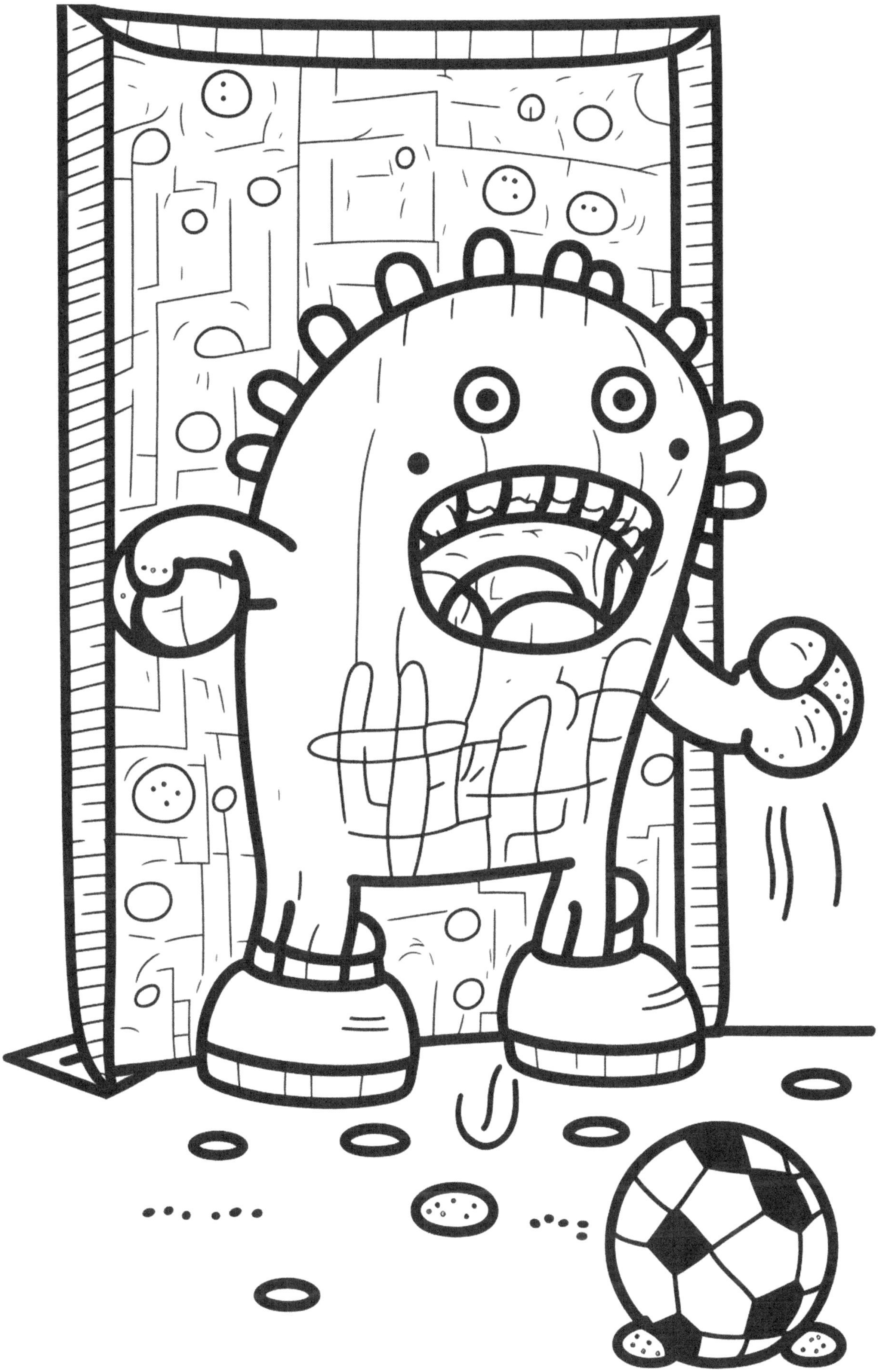

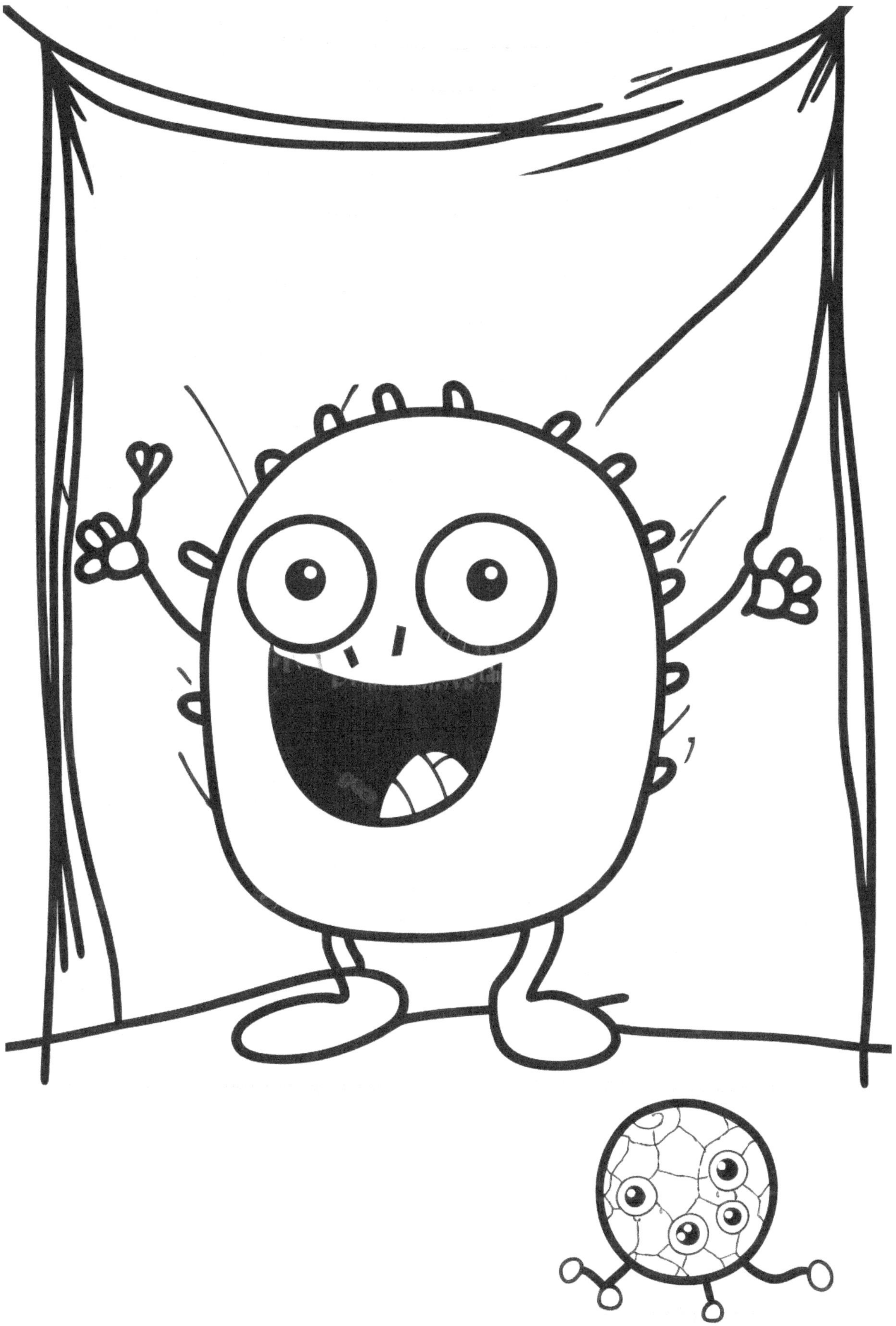

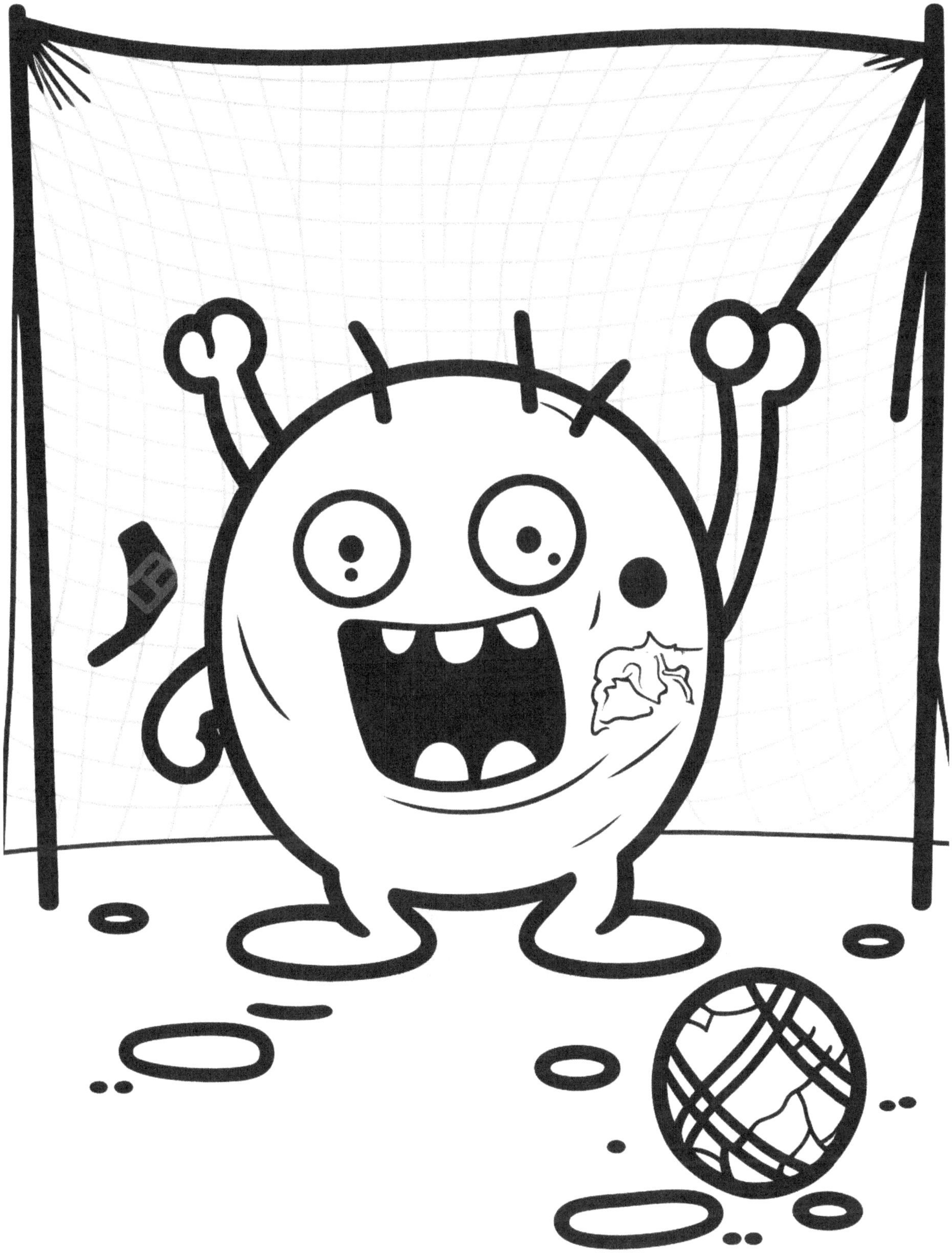

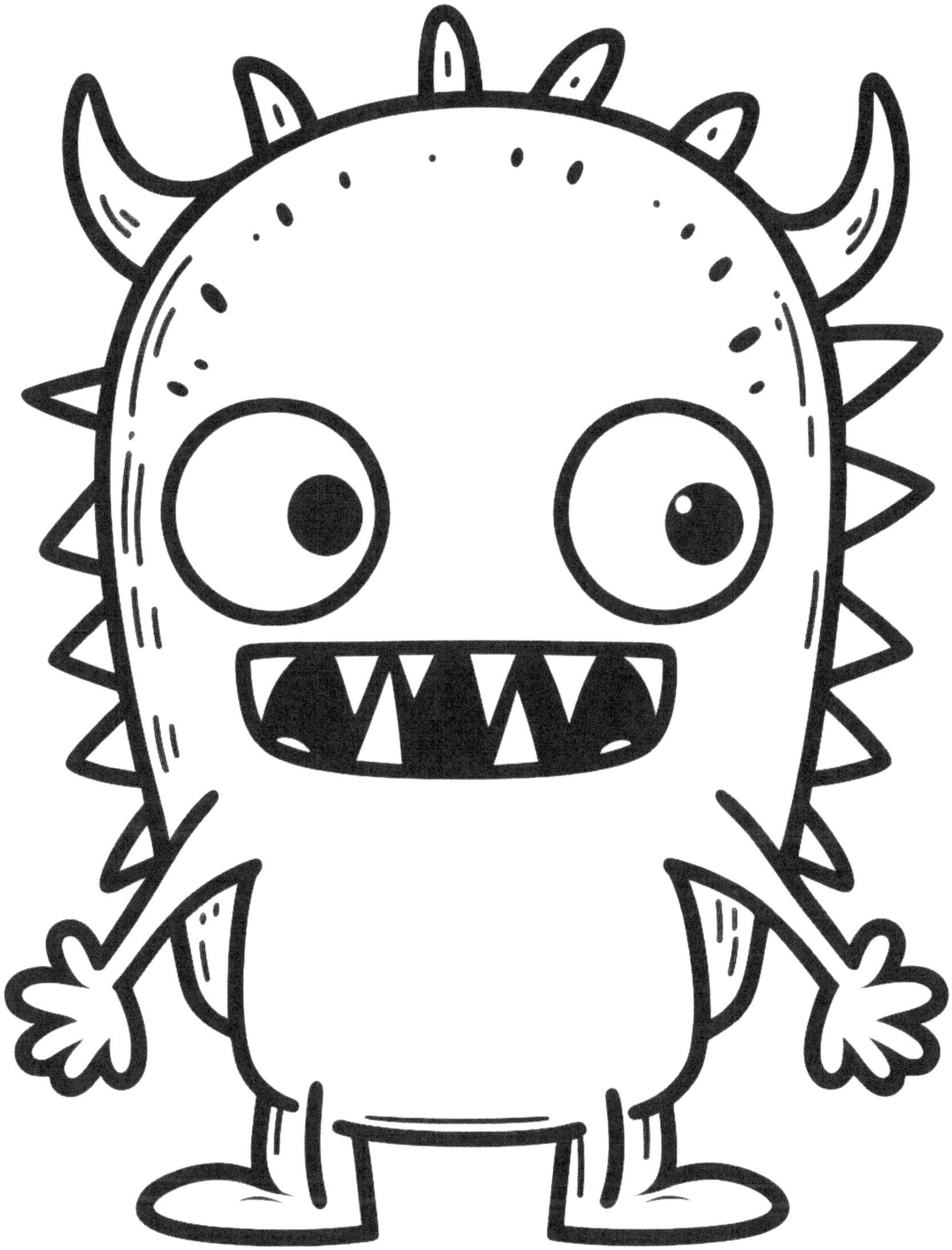

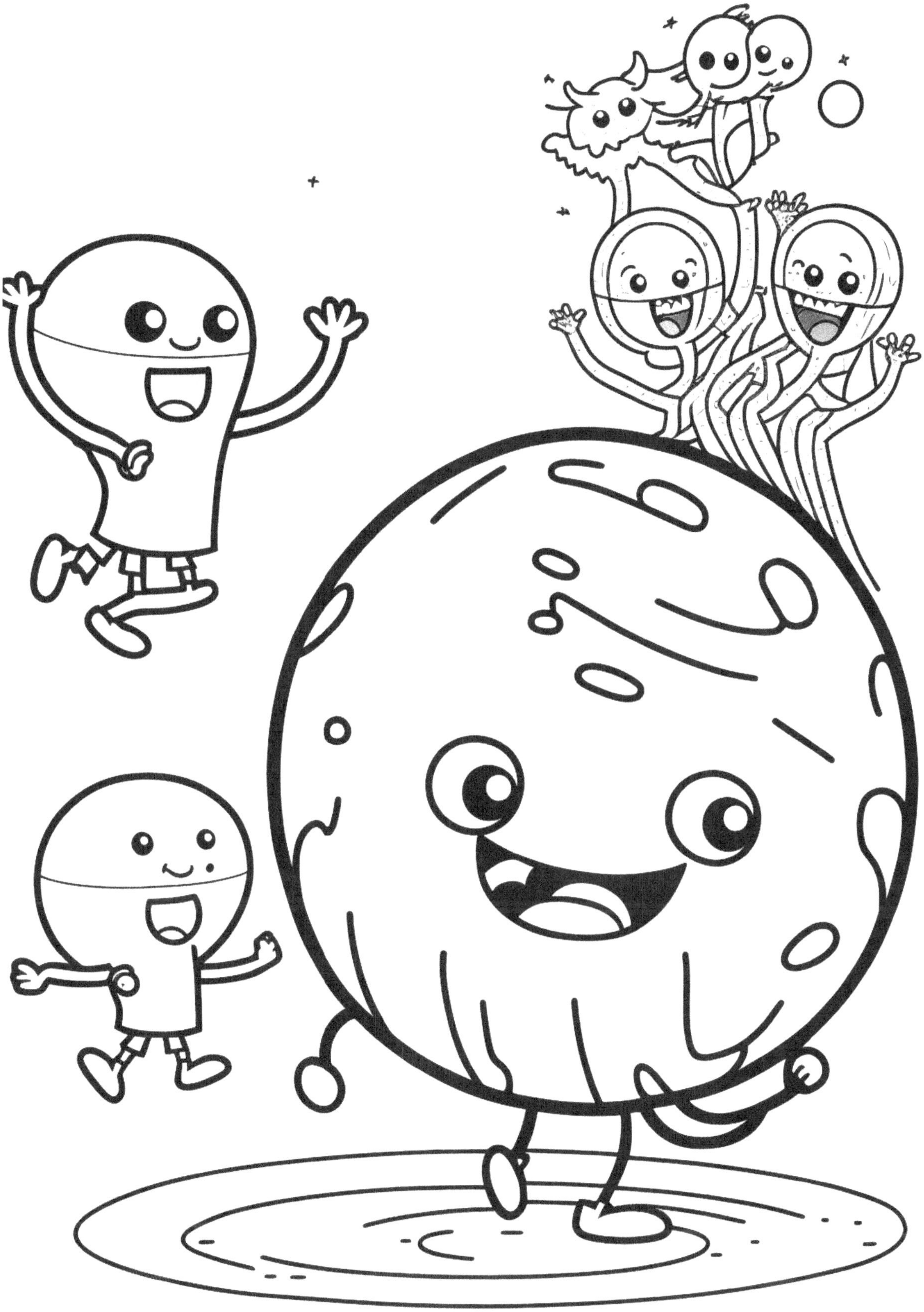

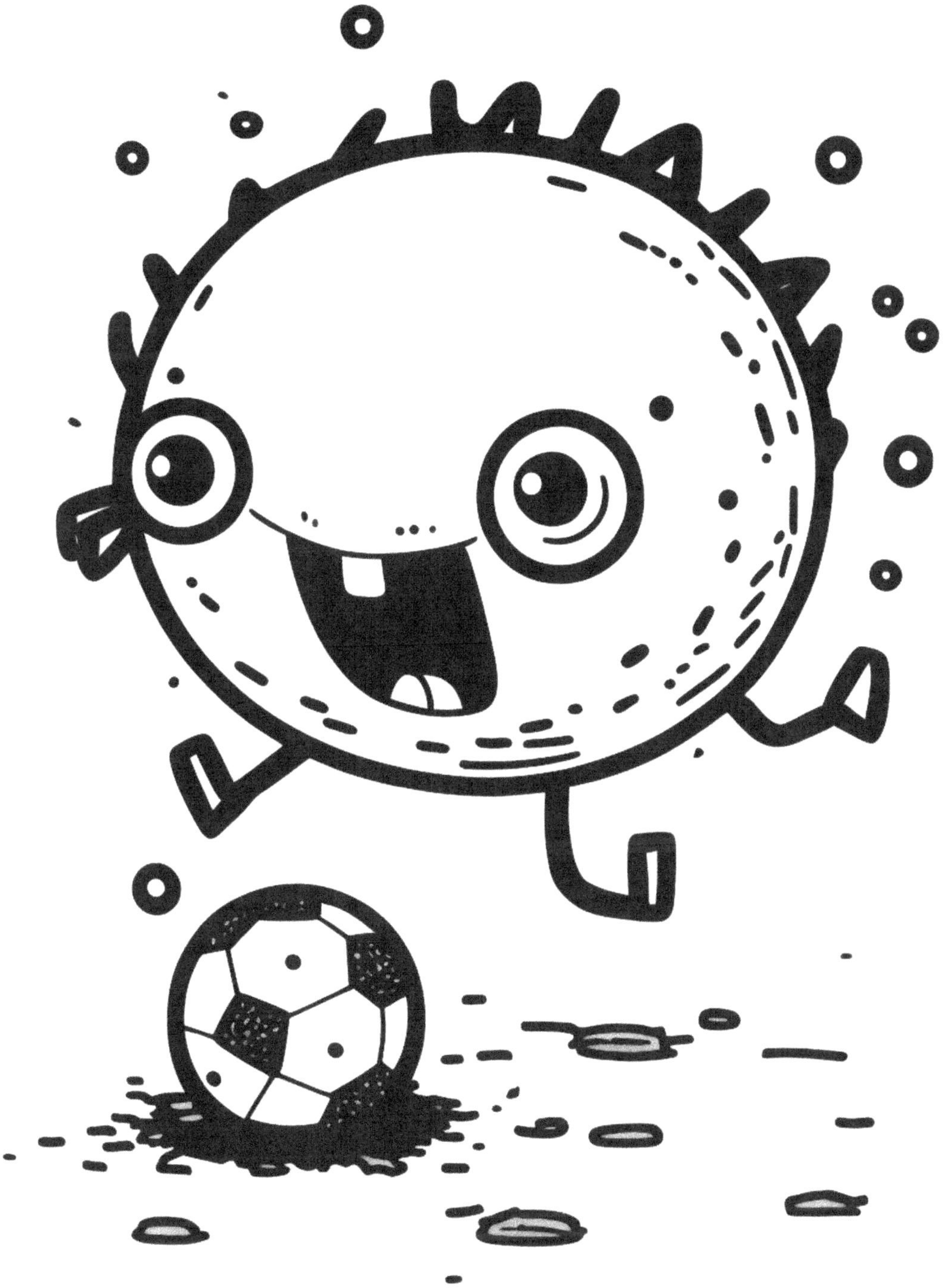

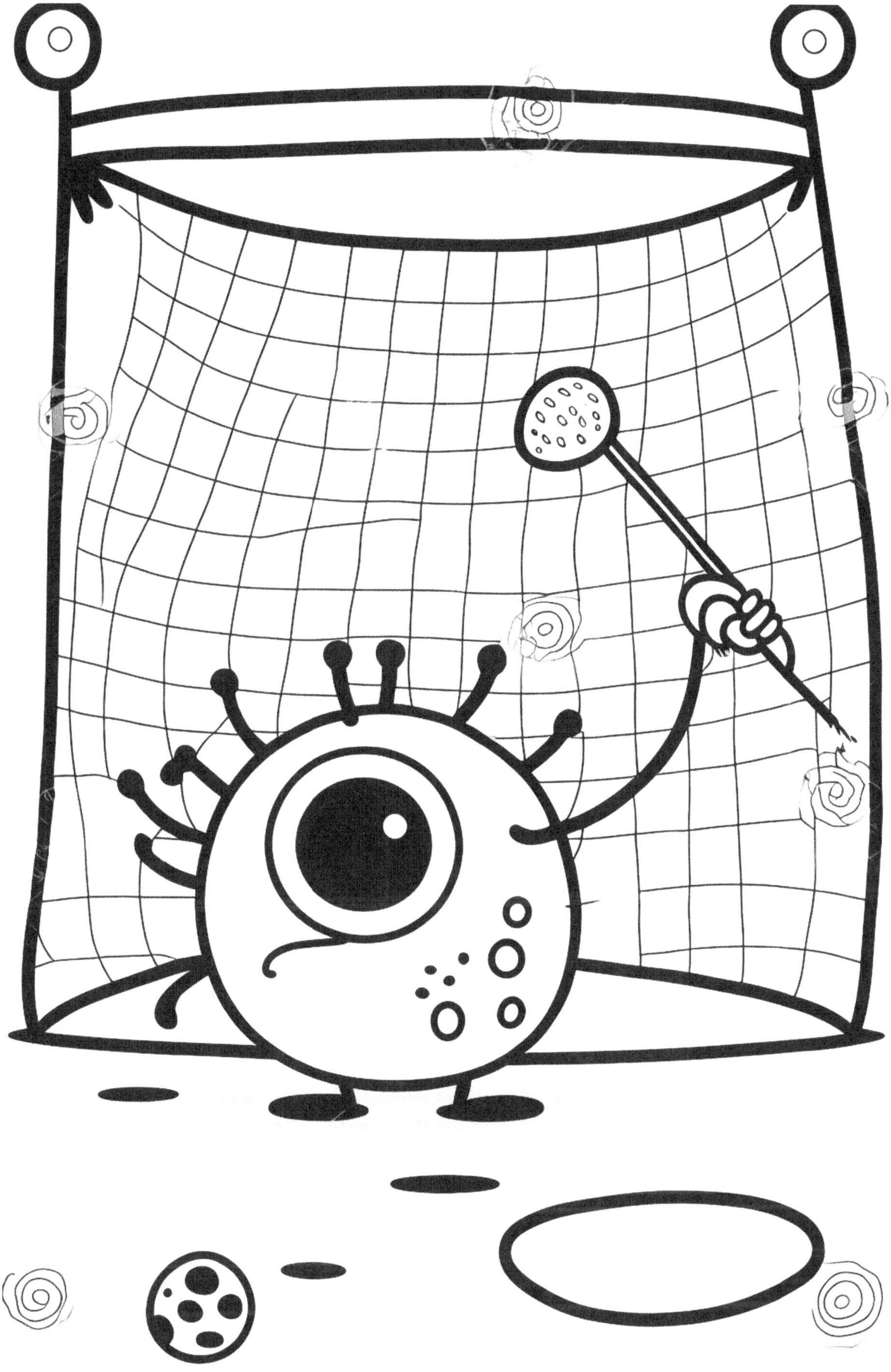

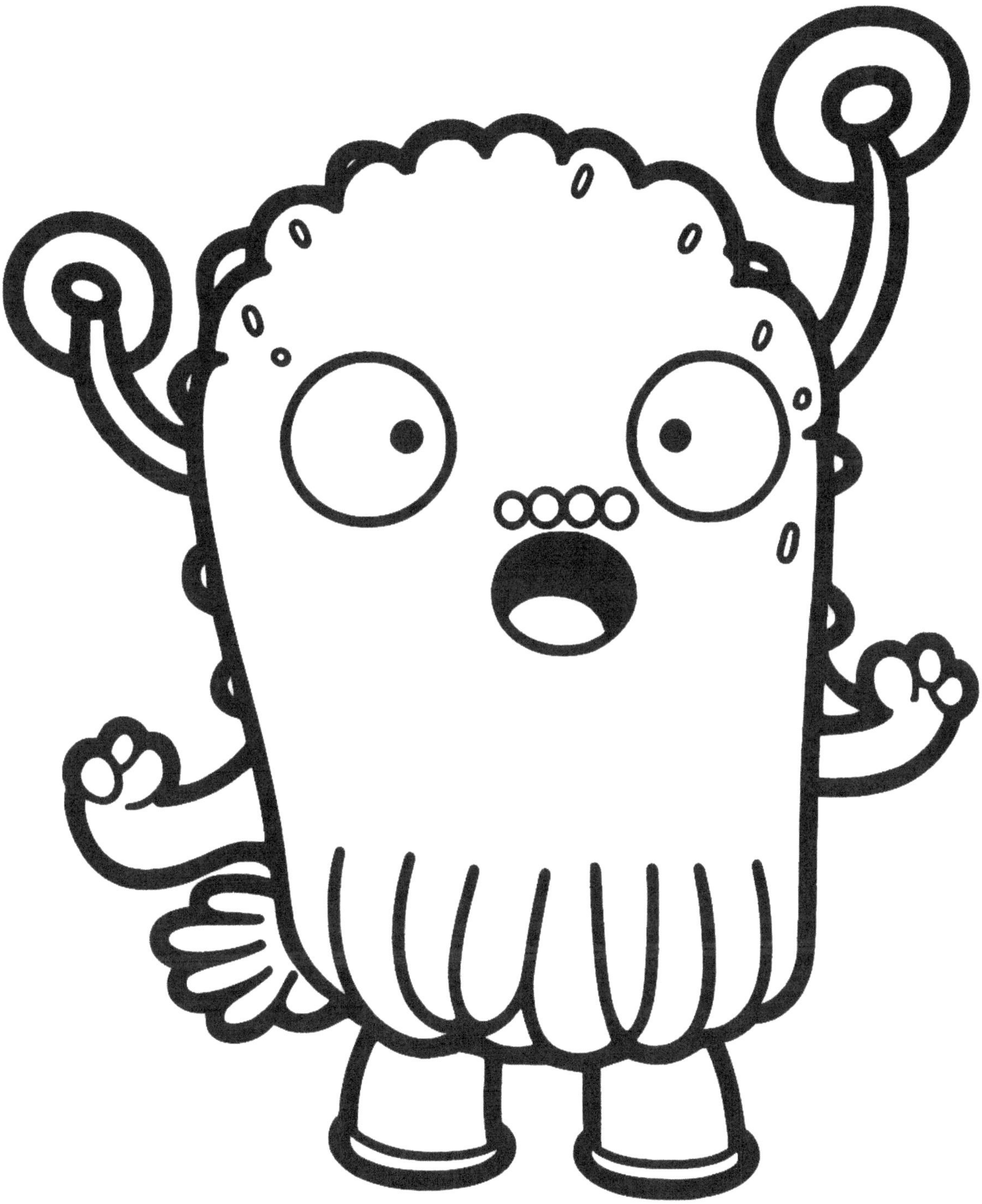

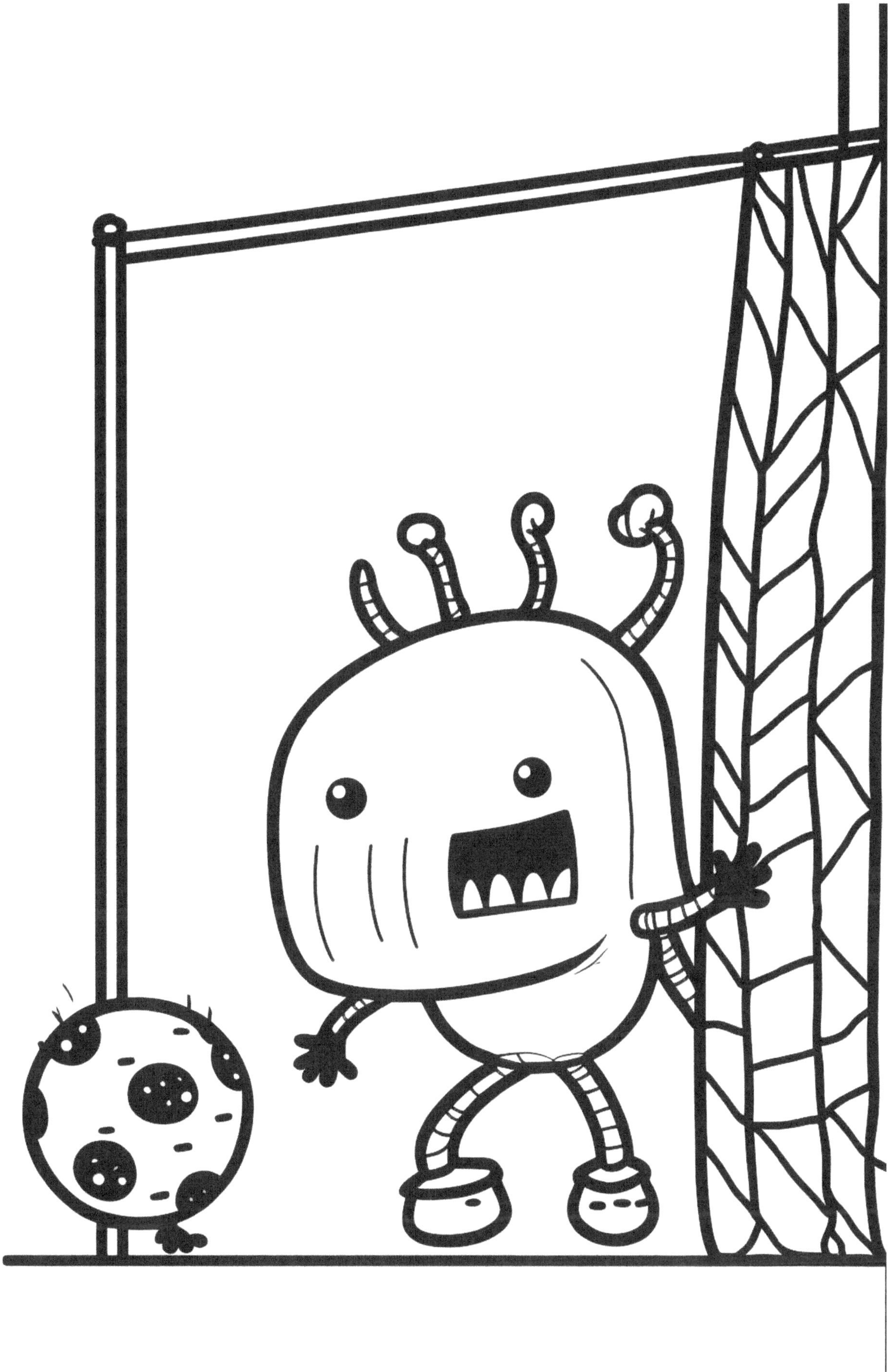

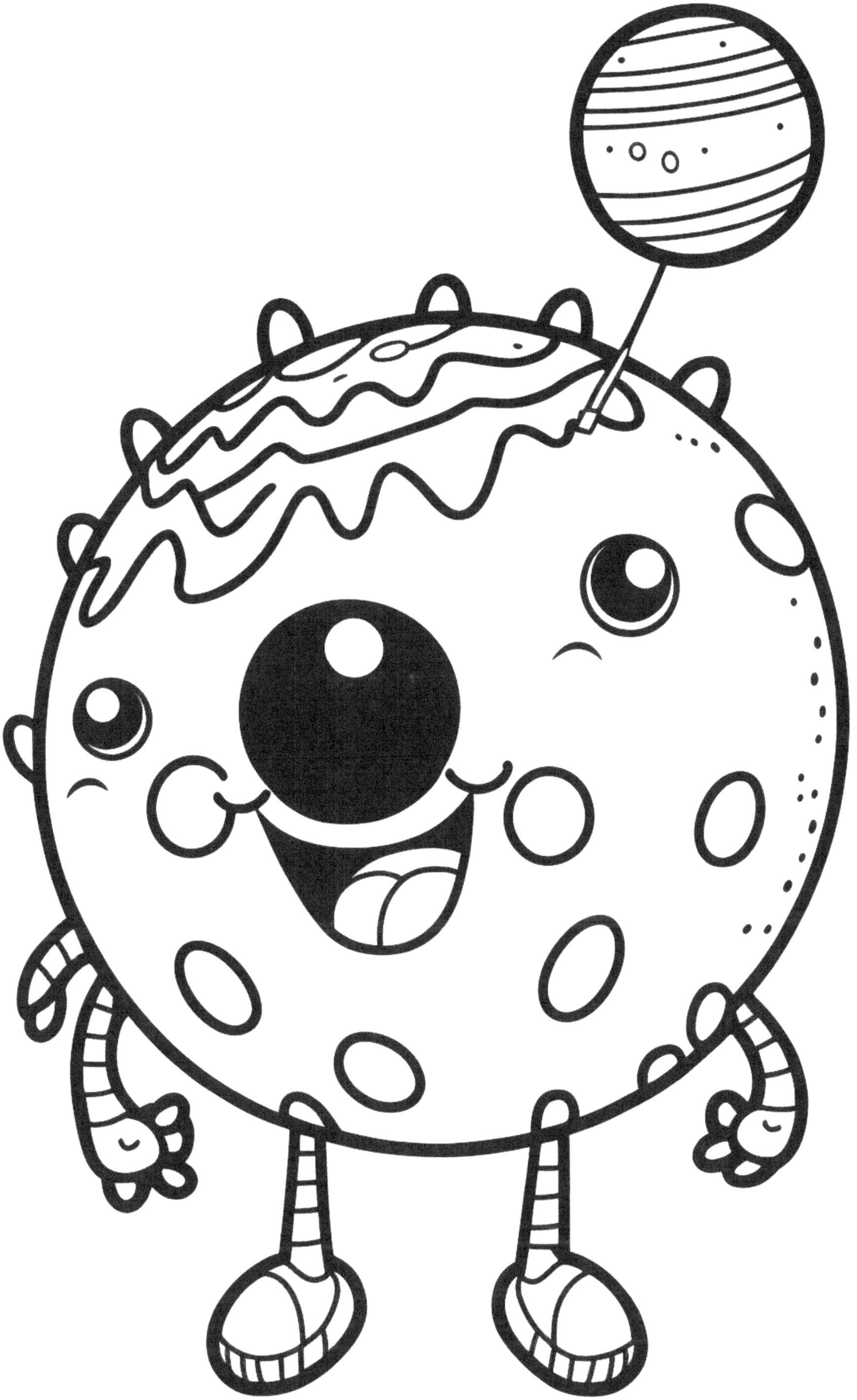

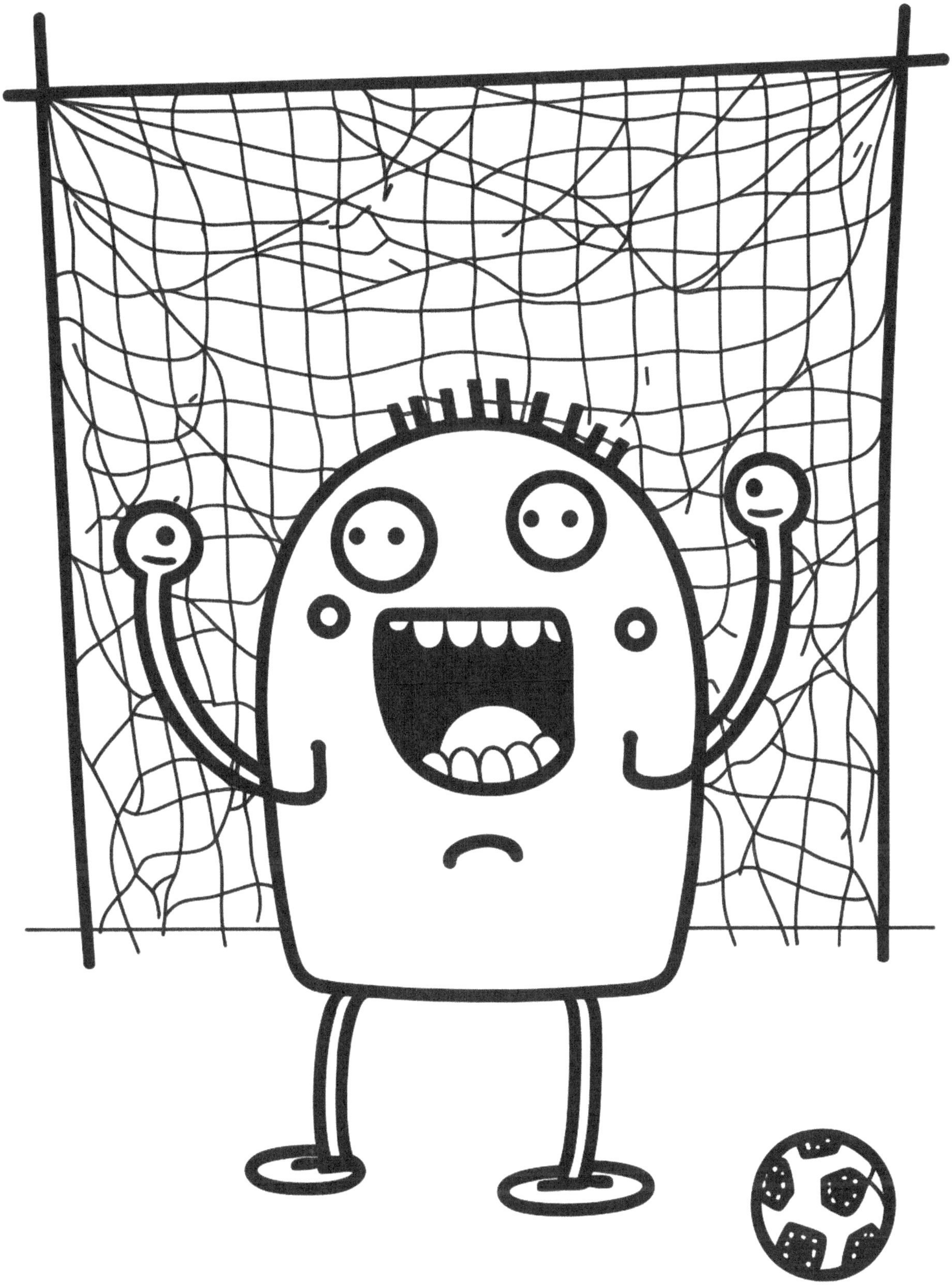

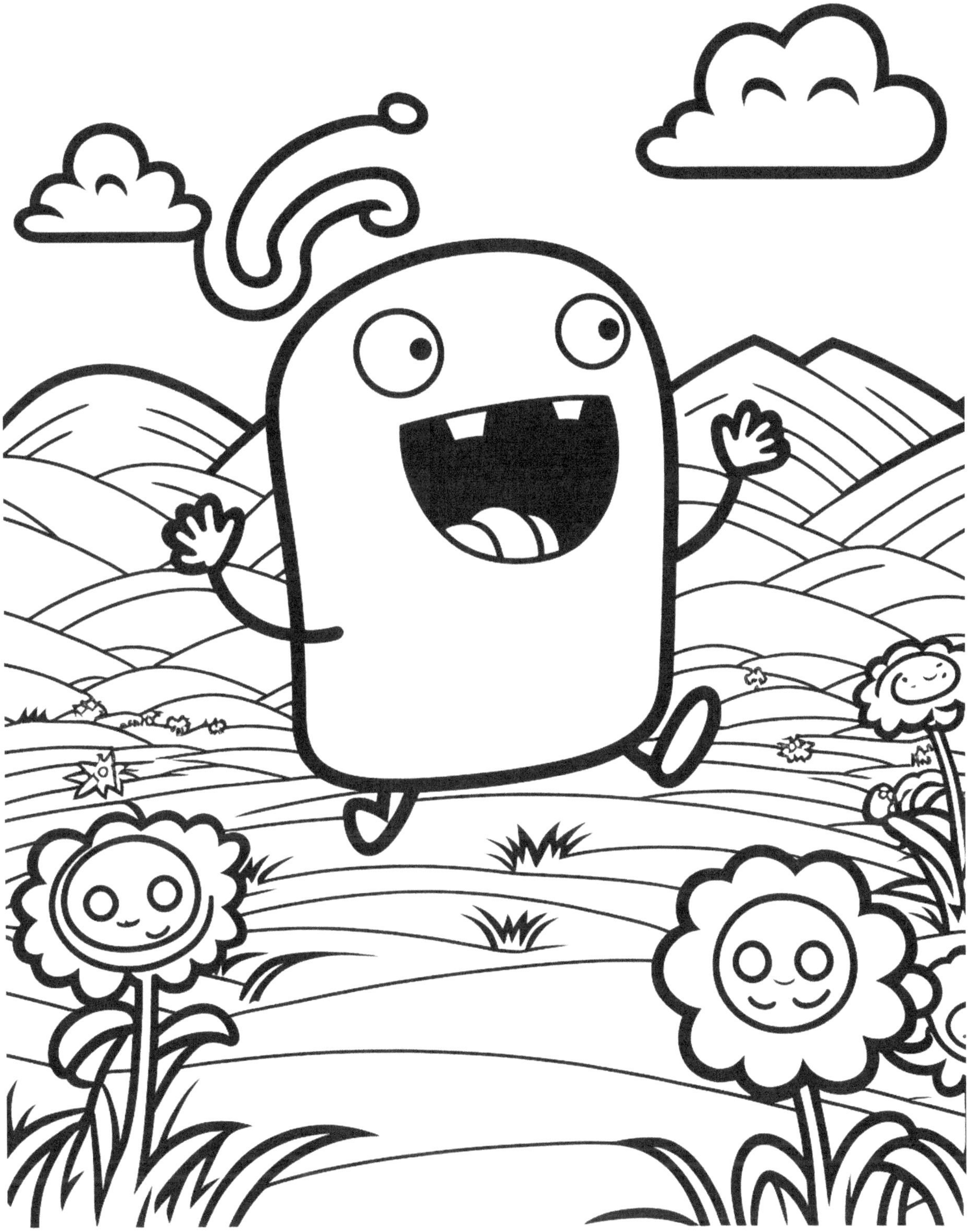

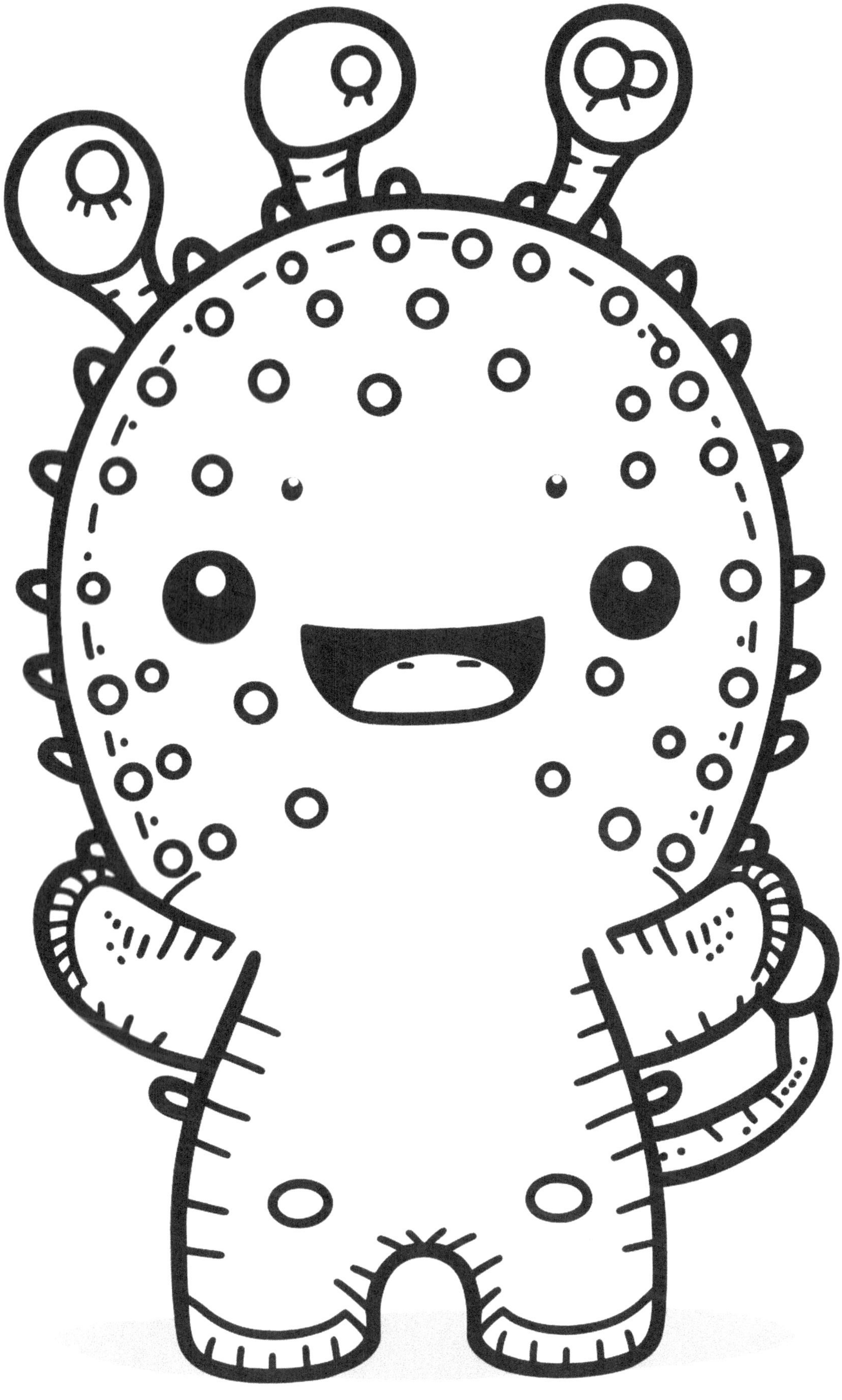

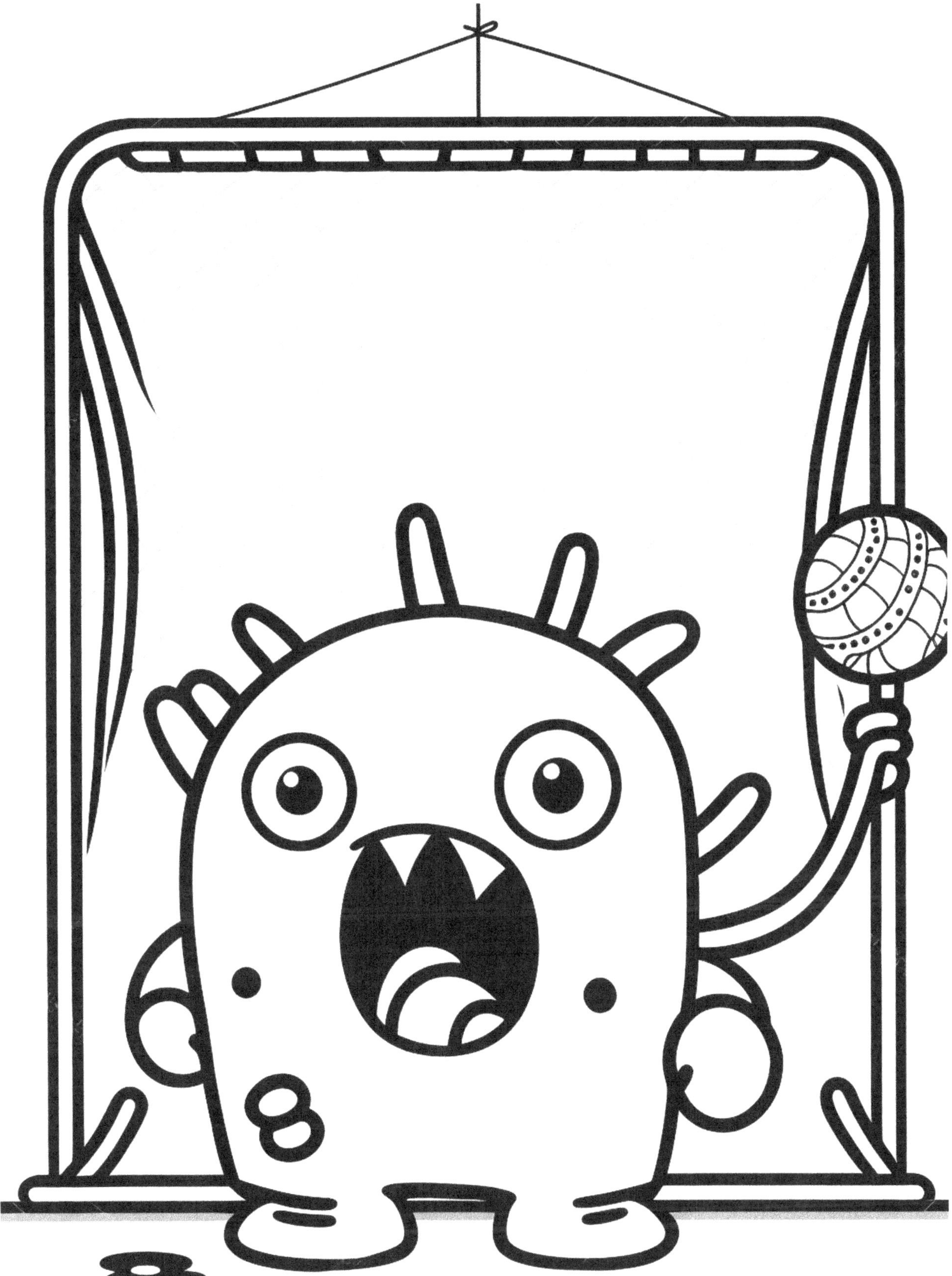

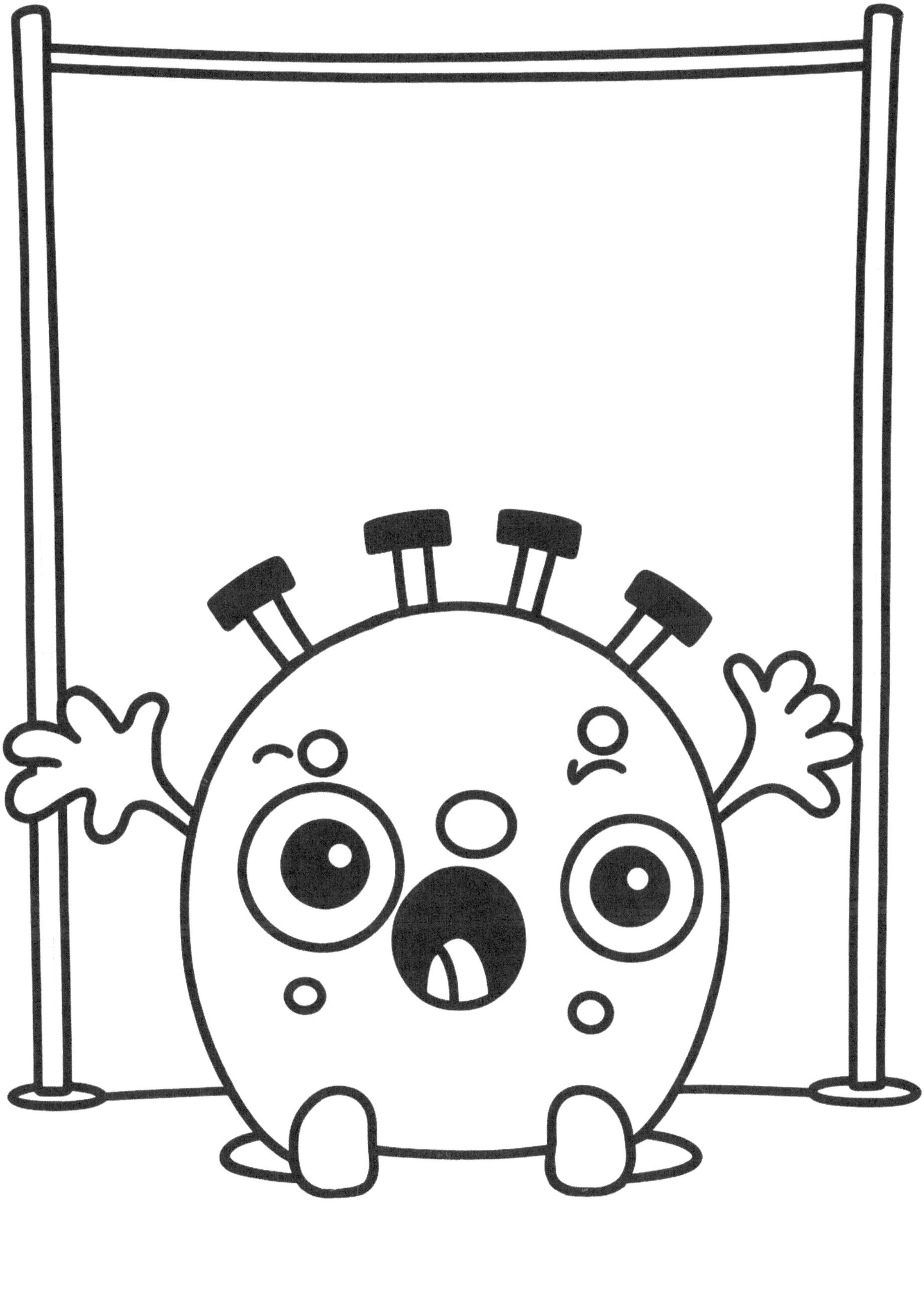

www.ingramcontent.com/pod-product-compliance
Lightning Source LLC
Chambersburg PA
CBHW060531010626
45794CB00023B/3305
9798871979761